This Is What
Democracy Looks Like

This Is What Democracy Looks Like

Essays on American Politics

Eric Leif Davin

DavinBooks
P.O. Box 90087
Pittsburgh, PA 15224

This Is What
Democracy Looks Like
Essays on American Politics

Dedication:

For Those Fighting for Democracy

Contents

Democracy in Danger

On a Sunday morning TV talk show shortly after the 2018 midterm elections I heard Dan Crenshaw, a newly elected Republican U. S. Representative from Texas, who was also an Afghanistan war veteran with a distinctive piratical eye patch, dispute the assertion of a Democratic guest that democracy was in danger. The Democrat was so taken-aback by his denial of what seemed obvious that he couldn't think of a rebuttal in the short time he had before the discussion moved on.

None of us participating in a live political discussion have time to deliver a dissertation on this subject (although the subject deserves one) before the discussion moves on. There are a host of things we could say about the state of democracy in contemporary America, from attacks on an independent press to attacks on an independent judiciary, but we have to be short and succinct in order to get anything across at all. So, here it is, the one issue at the heart of the matter:

The very meaning of the Greek word, "democracy," is "rule by the people." If the people don't have any say in who rules, that is the very negation of democracy.

And that is exactly what the Republicans have been trying to do for decades through voter suppression: Deny people any say in who rules.

They have been doing this through gerrymandering, in order to minimize Democratic voting power.

They have done it through the passage of numerous voter ID laws passed to eliminate "voter fraud," which does not exist in any significant form.

They did this when, four days before Election Day in 2018, Georgia officials, led by the Republican gubernatorial candidate (who was also the Georgia Secretary of State) put over 53,000 voter applications on hold via the state's "exact signature match" verification program. An estimated 70% of these were African Americans. (The Republican candidate ended up winning the election against the African American Democratic candidate by less than that number.)

They did this when North Dakota Republican officials passed a voter ID law mandating a street address on IDs. This was designed to limit the number of Native Americans living on reservations (which don't have street addresses) who could vote. In 2012 Democrat Heidi Heitkamp narrowly won her Senate seat in North Dakota with massive Native American support. Republicans were determined to eliminate this base of her support, and it worked. In 2018 Heitkamp lost her seat.

They did this in Kansas in 2018 when Republican officials moved the single voting place for the town of Dodge City, once the home of Sheriff Wyatt Earp, to a spot outside the town and a mile's walk from the nearest bus stop. They did this because Dodge City had become majority-Latino, and Latinos tended to vote Democratic.

All of these were fundamental attacks on the very concept of "democracy." So, is democracy in danger in contemporary America?

Yes, it is.

The Outlawed Vote

Anarchists are fond of disdainfully saying, "If voting changed anything, it would be outlawed." If that's the case, then voting must be able to change a lot of things, because the Powers That Be have outlawed voting for entire groups throughout the history of both the world and our country.

Mass democracy, in which all adult citizens can vote, is a very recent development. Most of human history is the history of kings, emperors, czars, and pharaohs, in which ordinary people are missing in action. We are told that the first emperor of China built the Great Wall of China, but I doubt he did any physical labor on it. We are told the Pharaoh Cheops built the Great Pyramid that bares his name, but I'm sure he never helped pull any great stone block into place. No, the ordinary people who actually built the pyramids and all the myriad human societies are lost in the abyss of time, because they had no say in what went on in their societies. They had no vote.

Even the famous ancient democracies were not actually democracies as we think of them. Women, of course, comprising at least half the population, had no legal say in any political decision anywhere at anytime until the 20th century. Further, ancient Athens, that "cradle of democracy", was a slave society, as were all ancient civilizations. Thus, slaves, who comprised a majority of the Athenian population, could not vote. Only the free adult males, a minority of the population, had any say in Athenian democracy.

It was much the same in the Roman Republic, which was actually the Roman Oligarchy. And that oligarchy kept a tight grip on its power. The oligarchs, for example, crucified the legendary Spartacus, who led a rebellion of enslaved gladiators. And "the noble Brutus," who led the Senatorial conspiracy to murder Julius Caesar in the name of the Republic, was exactly that, a nobleman Senator hoping to retain the oligarchic grip on political power. When they failed to do so, what followed was two thousand years of emperors and kings. And when the anonymous masses of ordinary people raised their voices in riot or revolt, because they had no votes, they were slaughtered and forgotten.

Things were a little better with the founding of America. The first colonies on the Atlantic shore of the new continent were so far from home that there was little the king back home in England could do to control the colonists. They were left to their own devices, like the tribe of children lost on the island in *The Lord of the Flies*.

But, even in Colonial America, as in *The Lord of the Flies,* the Big Boys dominated.

Women, of course, half the population, had no voice and no vote in Colonial legislatures.

Nor did slaves, and, in the beginning, there were slaves in every colony. Indeed, in South Carolina they were the majority.

Nor did indentured servants have a voice and a vote, even if they were white males.

Nor did even free white males who did not own land have a voice and a vote.

American democracy was hardly any democracy that we would recognize today. Only free white males who were landed proprietors had any say,

12

any vote, in the Colonial legislatures, only they knew what was best for everyone else.

American democracy, as we think of it today, took centuries of struggle to construct. For instance, it took the American Revolution, a long and violent war against the Mother Country in the name of "liberty," to change things for some. Having fought for freedom for eight long years, common ordinary men demanded a say, a vote, in how things were done. And so property requirements for voting were abolished in colony after colony, now states, for free white men.

It took another war, the Civil War, the bloodiest war in our history, to abolish slavery and give black men (but not black women) the right to vote...in theory. In practice, excessive poll taxes, intricate literacy tests, "grandfather clauses," and the night riding Ku Klux Klan kept them from voting.

It took the longest reform crusade in our history, from the Seneca Falls Convention in 1848 to 1920, for women to win the right to vote, to have a say in their own destinies.

And only in the 1920s did Native Americans win the right of citizenship in the land they had inhabited for thousands of years.

And it took another great crusade, the Civil Rights Movement of the 1950s and early 1960s, for African Americans to make real the right to vote they had been promised a hundred years earlier.

None of these were quixotic crusades, nor were they fools' errands. These struggles for the vote were real struggles for real power. This is because, in a democracy, there is only one way to have a voice in how society is governed, and that is by voting.

The oligarchs would like to speak with a loud voice in saying how society is governed, and they would like the mass of ordinary people to remain mute. This is why the oligarchs resisted for so long and so viciously. They believe they are the only ones who should have a share of power.

But, in politics there are never unalloyed victories and there are never permanent victories. The struggle goes on, because power never sleeps.

Power continues to gerrymander voting districts in order to curtail the voice of minorities.

Power continues to pass laws making it difficult for Native Americans on reservations to vote.

Power continues to pass laws curtailing the use of absentee and provisional ballots.

Power continues to pass laws cutting the number of polling places in minority districts and moving the remaining ones to inaccessible locations.

Power continues to pass laws forbidding prisoners who have served their time and who have returned to society as rehabilitated citizens from ever voting again.

Power continues to pass laws purging voting rolls and mandating proofs of citizenship.

Power continues to do whatever it can to outlaw voting for as many people as possible in whatever way possible.

Power does everything it can to outlaw voting because voting changes things.

Demographics Are Destiny

Why are Republicans so intent on curtailing electoral participation in America? The answer is: Demographics. Demographics are political destiny, and the long-term demographic tide is running against the Republicans. This is why they are so fearful of being "replaced."

Since its founding in the years before the Civil War, the Republican Party has always been America's white bread party, the party of native whites. When racial and ethnic minorities were just that, minorities, Republicans did well. But now America is heading toward "minority majority" status in the near future; that is, a majority of Americans are going to belong to minorities of one kind or another. And, mostly because of the Republican Party's long history of hostility toward racial and ethnic minorities, these minorities tend to vote Democratic.

For example, black Americans now constitute about 13% of the population, and even before Barack Obama ran for the presidency in 2008, 90% of black voters voted Democratic. That is not likely to change.

But, Republicans have problems with other minority voters as well. Asians, for instance, accounted for less than 1% of the population in 1960. In 2010, they accounted for 6%. Further, they are now the fastest growing demographic group, having passed Hispanics for that distinction, and are expected to account for 8% of the population by 2030. While Asians are not as overwhelmingly Democratic in their voting as black voters, a majority of Asian voters do vote Democratic. In the 2012 election, for example, Republican Mitt Romney garnered only 47% of the Asian vote.

The situation of Hispanics is more dramatic. In 1960 Hispanics represented only 3.6% of the population. In 2010 they represented 16.3% of the population, a larger percentage than black Americans. Demographers predict that by 2030 Hispanics will account for more than a fifth of all Americans, 22.5%. Historically, the majority of Hispanic voters have voted Democratic.

Meanwhile, the percentage of non-Hispanic white Americans is shrinking and, in 2013, reached a historic all-time low of 63% of the population. Demographers predict that whites will be a minority of Americans by 2050. Indeed, for some states and cities, that has already happened. Right now whites are minorities in four states: Texas, New Mexico, California, and Hawaii, plus the District of Columbia. Whites are also soon predicted to be a minority in Florida. By 2035 whites are predicted to also be a minority in Arizona, New Jersey, and perhaps New York and Delaware.

Further, 25 cities, including some of the biggest (New York, Los Angeles, Chicago, Houston, Phoenix, Buffalo, Tampa, Memphis, Cincinnati) have already reached minority majority status. And these minority majorities are increasingly voting Democratic.

Meanwhile, the majority of the white population, which is shrinking all the time, votes Republican. (This is due primarily to the large majority of white males who vote Republican. The majority of white women have voted Democratic for decades, with that percentage increasing.) In 2012,

16

white voters accounted for 90% of Mitt Romney's votes. Indeed, in 2012 Obama was the first presidential candidate in history to lose the white vote by double digits – but he still won the White House. This is because the white vote is translating into fewer electoral collage votes with each election.

In 1988 George H. W. Bush won 59% of the white vote, which translated into 426 electoral college votes. In 2012 Romney also won 59% of the white vote, which translated into 206 electoral college votes. Clearly, as with Barack Obama, no future Democratic presidential candidate needs a majority of the white vote to win the White House.

The rise of the ideology of white supremacy in the Republican Party can only hasten the realignment of racial and ethnic voters into the Democratic Party. This is why the Republican Party has become a white racist, anti-democratic, authoritarian political party. Indeed, it has become a fascist political party.

Fascism & Fascists

Hey, kids! Let's learn two new and useful words that you can use everyday with your friends and the people with whom you associate! These words are "fascism" and "fascist." Perhaps you've already heard them. But, what do they mean?

"Fascism" is an authoritarian, anti-democratic political ideology or movement that that believes in using violence, or the threat of violence, to further its racist, nationalist agenda and to silence and suppress its political opponents. A "fascist," therefore, is someone who believes in this ideology, or participates in this movement.

This word is so useful in everyday conversation today because fascism is alive and well in America and there are probably fascists all around you. Perhaps your neighbor is a fascist. Perhaps there are fascists in your very own family!

So, these are handy words to describe those neighbors or family members, and the ideas and positions they advocate. Now you can use them with confidence.

Sedition

Hey, kids, now let's talk about a useful word you can use in everyday situations in today's complicated political world, especially after the 2021 attack by the Trumpist mob on our nation's Capitol. Was that attack on the heart of our democracy an act of sedition? You betcha!

Some folks referred to the attack on Congress as it met to perform a crucial legal ritual in the constitutional and peaceful transfer of political authority from one presidential administration to another by different words. Some described it as a "failed coup" or an "attempted insurrection." Yes, those phrases certainly apply, but it was also an act of "sedition." But, what does that word mean, exactly?

The current federal criminal code defines sedition, in part, as an effort by two or more people "to oppose by force the authority [of the government of the United States], or by force to prevent, hinder or delay the execution of any law of the United States, or by force to seize, take or possess any property of the United States contrary to the authority thereof."

Does this describe the Trumpist mob's attack on our Capitol in an attempt "by force to prevent, hinder or delay the execution of any law of the United States"? It sure does! The assault was meant to halt the legal and constitutionally mandated counting of the presidential Electoral College vote. That certainly meets the legal definition of sedition!

In addition, the Trumpist mob certainly seized and took possession of property of the United States government. It not only seized the heart of our democracy, the Capitol building itself, including both the Senate chamber and the chamber of the House of Representatives, it also seized House Majority Leader Nancy Pelosi's office and walked off with her podium and her laptop. Federal law enforcement officers later arrested over 850 members of the Trumpist mob, including those who occupied her office and stole her podium and laptop.

So, the Trumpist mob's attack on Congress was an "attempted coup," a "failed insurrection," and also an act of "sedition," all of those things...and most specifically an act of sedition.

So, there you have it kids! Now you know how to describe exactly, appropriately, and legally the actions of the Trumpist mob during its attack on the heart of our democracy. Sedition! Use the word today in your next conversation!

Populism:
America's Ideology

After Donald Trump's electoral victory in 2016, populism suffered a lot of abuse at the hands of political pundits and Sunday morning talk show hosts. A prominent critic was Fareed Zakaria, a *Washington Post* columnist and sometime essayist for *TIME*. Zakaria's most visible current attack on populism was an article titled, "Populism on the March: Why the West is in Trouble," published immediately after Trump's election in the November-December, 2016 issue of *Foreign Affairs*. His article set the tone for much punditry thereafter. This fear and distrust of populism among the elites has a long history, going back at the very least to the 1950s, when liberal intellectuals decried the demagoguery of Senator Joseph McCarthy.

What all these media commentators seemingly fail to understand with their trash talk against populism is that populism is not a strange aberration of democracy that rears its ugly head during times of crisis. Broadly speaking, populism is the belief that the will of the people should prevail over the will of privileged elites. Thus, populism is the concept of democracy itself, and elite fears of populism are actually fears of democracy. This fear of democracy has a tradition in this country that goes back to our founding as a nation when the Founders wrote the Constitution to curtail what they saw as the dangers of too much democracy.

Nor is populism the monolithic philosophy these commentators portray. It can be manifested as what might be called "Right Populism," as exemplified by Donald Trump, and is the version of populism these pundits fear and decry. But it can also be manifested as "Left Populism," as exemplified by Bernie Sanders. Both versions are powerful. In the 2016 primaries, Donald Trump garnered 13.3 million votes with his version of Right Populism. But Bernie Sanders garnered almost as many votes, 13 million, with his version of a Left Populism that promised "A Future To Believe In," and he won 22 states, including states that Hillary Clinton lost in the general election, such as Indiana, Wisconsin, and Michigan.

Left Populism is a protest tradition, one that champions the common people against the rich and powerful, that has always been America's dominant ideology of dissent. Most American radicals, including working class radicals, have commonly thought of themselves as "the people " instead of "the workers," even though they may have been of the working class. Given the dominance of Left Populism in American protest thought, it should surprise no one that the all-time best-selling history of American radicalism, with well over one million copies in print, celebrates America's Left Populist heritage. It is, of course, Howard Zinn's "*A People's History of the United States.*"

Before the radical upsurge of the 1960s, the other great period of twentieth century protest was the 1930s. Despite what the Left might wish to believe about the legendary labor upheavals of the 1930s, it was Left Populism, not some variant of Marxism, that mobilized "the workers" in that earlier period of radicalism. Indeed, the labor struggles of the Thirties were part of a wider Left Populist movement at that time for inclusion of the downtrodden in the American Dream. This is why they rallied to President Franklin D. Roosevelt and made the Democratic Party the majority party in the New Deal Era. Journalist Bill Moyers recalls that FDR seemed to be the champion of all the "Forgotten Men" who were "Lost in America," the entire dispossessed and tossed aside.

Bill Moyers was raised a Baptist in East Texas where his father had left school after the fourth grade to begin life as a cotton picker. His father bought a radio with his meager savings just so he could listen to FDR, "the aristocrat speaking up for common people," during his "Fireside Chats." And the message of FDR and his New Deal, said Moyers, the message his father heard coming over that radio in the East Texas cotton fields was this: "Class and power were not fixed by Nature; inequality was wrong and unemployment humiliating; runaway capitalism could be tamed, privilege checked, monopolies broken up, an end put to government by organized money. To people down and out, broken and feeling betrayed, Roosevelt talked of democracy. He made them think they had a stake in it and a responsibility for it."

The common people Moyers spoke of embodied a down-to-earth, blue collar, multi-ethnic, populist ideal we find elsewhere in popular culture during the Thirties. This ideal is found, for instance, in the thousands of photos taken by the photographers sent out across America by the Farm Security Administration (FSA). From 1935 to 1943 Roy Stryker directed a team of some twenty FSA photographers who produced over 270,000 pictures of America's "common people." Stryker's photographers took some of the iconic images we have of the Great Depression, such as Dorothea Lange's "Okie Madonna", an impoverished woman broken down somewhere in a California farm field with her children hanging onto her.

The reason these photos are so populist is because Roy Stryker deliberately sought pictures of "the common people," the hard working survivors who built America. "I think it's significant," Stryker later said, "that in our entire collection we have only one picture of Franklin Roosevelt, the most newsworthy man of the era -- this, mind you, in a collection that's sometimes said to have reported the feel and smell and taste of the Thirties even more vividly than the news media.... you'll find no record of big people or big events in the collection.... not a single shot of Wall Street, and absolutely no celebrities."

This ideal was in the air. In 1936, in what he termed his own favorite poem, Carl Sandburg celebrated "The People, Yes!" In 1941, Pulitzer Prize-winning poet Stephen Vincent Benet urged us to "Listen To The People." These people included, "Paul Bunchick and the Greek who runs the Greek's/ The black-eyed children out of Sicily/ All of them there and all of them a nation. / Our voice is not one voice, but many voices. / Not one man's, not the greatest, but the people's."

In 1942 Aaron Copeland wrote a hymn of praise to "the common man" in his "Lincoln Portrait," the most stirring portion of which is his triumphant beginning, the "Fanfare for the Common Man." Copeland has a reader quote passages from Abraham

24

Lincoln to the accompaniment of stirring music, passages such as "The spirit of slavery is the same as the spirit that says, 'You work and toil and earn bread, and I'll eat it.' No matter in what shape it comes, whether from a mouth of a king, or from one race of men as an apology for enslaving another race, it is the same tyrannical principle." This was a theme also commonly expressed by radical labor unions in the Thirties, such as the Independent Textile Union of Rhode Island, which had approvingly published the very same Lincoln passage five years before in a 1937 issue of its newspaper.

But perhaps the musical genre that most closely reflected the spirit of the times was folk music. Americans have long composed and sung "traditional" songs such as cowboy laments, Delta blues, Kentucky bluegrass, and the hillbilly songs of Appalachia, with their roots in Elizabethan and Scots-Irish ballads. It was not until the twentieth century, however, that such songs came to be identified as "folk songs" of "the people," a populist musical genre that cohered in the 1930s. And it is no accident that the music we most closely identify with the Thirties is folk music, a genre which describes the lives, loves, and labors of the common people. It is also no accident, then, that the two periods that witnessed the proliferation of folk songs, the Thirties and the Sixties, were also the only two eras of the twentieth century that witnessed the emergence and flowering of significant and widespread populist and oppositional countercultures.

Even the obdurate Communist Party eventually adopted the Left Populism of the times with its 1935 "Popular Front" strategy. That year the party changed its official slogan to, "Communism is

Twentieth Century Americanism." Meanwhile, the volunteers it sent to fight in Spain against the fascists in that country's civil war did so as members of "The Abraham Lincoln Brigade." At the same time, the Communist-affiliated Composers Collective began including in its *Workers Song Books* indigenous folk music of all types, including songs of farmers, miners, urban workers, and African-Americans – songs of "the people." It should come as no surprise, therefore, that the Communist Party reached its most influence and its highest membership levels during this Popular Front period when it promoted Left Populism.

The most influential folk singer of the Thirties was no doubt Woody Guthrie. He was born into an impoverished Oklahoma dust bowl family and was closely associated with the Communist Party. Guthrie composed more than a thousand songs reflecting the decade's spirit of Left Populist protest. Perhaps his most well known song is "This Land is Your Land," which declared, "this land belongs to you and me," not, it suggested, to the rich and the corporations.

In 1941 Guthrie joined Pete Seeger, Lee Hays, and others to form the Almanac Singers, a popular folk group that sang for C.I.O. (Congress of Industrial Organizations) organizing campaigns and political rallies. After World War II, as America became more politically conservative, Guthrie, Seeger, and other members of the Almanac Singers kept the Left Populist spirit of folk music alive through such groups as People's Songs. It was at a meeting of the People's Songs Board of Directors that Pete Seeger and Lee Hays wrote "If I Had a Hammer," which gained widespread popularity in the early Sixties after the folk trio of Peter, Paul, and Mary made it a hit. In the song, Seeger and Hays proclaimed that they would hammer out justice and freedom "all over this land."

This Left Populist theme was also echoed in the films of Italian director Frank Capra, perhaps the most popular and successful film director of the 1930s, responsible for such films as "Mr. Smith Goes To Washington" and "Meet John Doe". Born in Sicily in 1897, Capra immigrated to Los Angeles with his parents in 1903. When America entered World War I, he joined the army. After the Armistice, Capra returned to Los Angeles, but was unable to find a job. He bummed around for several years, working at odd jobs, ending up down and out in San Francisco. It was during those days that Capra came to believe that, "The rich have it all, but accomplish little." The essence of Frank Capra's Left Populism, reflected in his subsequent films, was that it was the decent, hard-working, "little guy" who really represented all that was most American -- while the wealthy and the representatives of the powerful represented a venal corruption of the American ideal.

This struggle for more democracy – for more government of the people, by the people, and for the people, in the words of Abraham Lincoln at Gettysburg – is, and always has been, the central conflict of American politics. Yes, right-wing demagogues, such as Donald Trump, can hijack this struggle and pervert it into something to fear.

But it is also our only hope for "A Future To Believe In."

Balancing the Budget

Any time the federal government implements large programs to aid ordinary American citizens, Republicans in Congress and elsewhere raise a hue and cry about how this will increase the deficit. Instead, they say, we should be "balancing the budget."

Republicans never voice this faux concern when the military budget is increased, and thus increases the deficit, only when ordinary citizens might benefit from federal spending. Indeed, this hobgoblin has been so prevalent in American politics for so long that even Democratic presidents and presidential candidates, who should not be so easily bamboozled, have also raised the cry.

For instance, during the 1932 presidential campaign, in the midst of the Great Depression, the Democratic challenger, Franklin D. Roosevelt, came to old Forbes Field in Pittsburgh's Oakland neighborhood. There he unveiled the major pledge of his campaign. As president, he would "balance the budget."

As it happened, the economy was in such collapse it didn't matter what the Democratic challenger promised. He was guaranteed victory against the Republican incumbent, Herbert Hoover, seen as responsible for the economic shambles.

Once in office, FDR discovered the only way out of the economic mess he'd inherited was through a big government economic stimulus program. So, he funded a number of such programs, such as the Civilian Conservation Corps and the Works Progress Administration.

But, because FDR and most of Congress still believed the most important priority was "balancing the budget," none of these programs, known collectively as "The New Deal," were funded enough to completely pull the economy out of the Depression.

Yet they did bring about enough of a recovery so that things began to look better and, in 1936, the slight economic recovery helped FDR win a historic re-election landslide victory.

Encouraged by the margin of safety his re-election gave him, and the slight economic recovery, FDR decided it was now time to get serious about "balancing the budget." So, in his second term, he cut back on all the meager deficit stimulus spending he'd promoted.

The economy promptly relapsed into what historians call "The Roosevelt Recession" of 1937. His Republican opponents surged back to victory in the 1938 congressional mid-term elections and FDR's New Deal was effectively ended because he fell victim to the Republican demands to "balance the budget."

Meanwhile, the economy hobbled on to the end of the 1930s, only to be finally pulled out of the Great Depression by the massive government deficit spending required to militarily win World War II.

FDR never did fulfill his Pittsburgh Promise to "balance the budget" and stop deficit spending. But, the economy was booming -- and so no one cared about "balancing the budget" for many, many years.

Independent Voters & Primaries:
How It Works

In the wake of the 2016 New York Democratic presidential primary, in which Senator Bernie Sanders lost to Hillary Clinton, Bernie complained that three million Independent voters in New York state, many of whom may well have voted for him (as Independents did in other states) were "disenfranchised" because New York has "closed primaries." This is also true of Pennsylvania and many other states.

A "closed," as opposed to an "open," primary means that only members registered in a political party are permitted to vote in determining the candidates of that party. Thus, three million New York voters who were registered as "Independent" of any political party did not participate in that year's Democratic and Republican primary elections in New York. Bernie and his supporters viewed that as "unfair" and "undemocratic."

Let's discuss that.

First, some background:

The political system in the United States is a federal system. That means a lot of political authority is devolved to the states. One of the areas in which this is so is in the area of running elections. It is for this reason that the 50 states have primaries and caucuses on so many different dates. And it is for this reason that some states have open primaries, in which

Independents can vote, and other states have closed primaries, in which they cannot.

State law also governs deadlines for registering to vote or changing your party registration or registering in a party. In Pennsylvania, for example, the deadline for registering to vote or for changing your party registration, or changing from Independent into a party, is one month before the election in which you wish to vote.

In New York, the deadline for changing one's party registration, or changing from Independent into a party, is six months before the election in which you wish to vote. Thus, in New York, they had to do so in October of 2015, the year before the 2016 presidential primaries, and before anyone even had a good idea of who the candidates might have been. (For the record, I think that is unreasonable, with no logistical rationale, but that's the law in New York.) The two states have different deadlines because the federal devolution of political authority gives the states the authority to set their own rules for running their elections.

So, if you don't like the fact that Independents can't vote in a closed primary, or don't like the time frame for changing one's voting status, and you think such requirements disenfranchise Independents in some way – then change the law in your own state in this regard. Petitioning some one cannot do this. It can only be done in the way that all laws are made or unmade, by having the state legislature pass new laws or rescind old laws. This means you either lobby the elected state legislators to do so, or you elect new legislators more favorable to your position.

As to the rationale for closed primaries, it is as follows: Contrary to what many political neophytes believe, political parties are not public organizations, nor are they state entities. The Founders who wrote the Constitution said absolutely nothing about political parties in the Constitution, because there were no political parties in America in the 1780s when they were writing the Constitution, nor did they envision their future existence. Indeed, the first embryonic political parties, the Federalists and the Anti-Federalists, only sprang into existence during the debates over the ratification of the Constitution that were conducted *after* the Constitution was written. The Founders perhaps *should* have predicted this devlopment, but they did not. Rather, the appearance of political parties was an unintended consequence of the political structure the Founders created with the Constitution.

For example, take the fact that each Congressional district elects only one Representative. This means that anyone who gets 51% of the vote, or wins a plurality in the case of multiple candidates, gets 100% of the political power and the losing 49% of voters get zero percent of the political power. This also meant that organizations, political parties, appeared spontaneously once the Constitution went into effect in order to aggregate the vote of like-minded voters and win 51% of the vote.

Because political parties are not discussed in any way in the Constitution, they are not part of our constitutional political structure. Instead, they are private organizations, private political clubs, not government entities, which came into existence to operate under the rules of the game mandated by the Constitution. This is why the Democrats and

Republicans have such different rules for selecting their presidential delegates. The Republicans, for example, have winner-take-all primaries in some states, if the local state Republican Party in that state wants them, while the Democrats elect all of their delegates by proportional representation. As private political clubs they can decide how to structure their primaries in any way they wish.

In another example, in Pennsylvania the candidate allegiance of Democratic presidential delegates is listed on the ballot, so you know who the delegate you vote for will support. However, the Pennsylvania Republican Party has chosen to list all their presidential delegates as "uncommitted" on the ballot, so the Republican voter has no idea, as least from ballot listing, which delegate supports which candidate. Each party is free to decide the rules governing the election of its delegates because political parties are, as I said, private clubs, and, as such, they can operate by any rules they wish.

It follows from this that the members of these private clubs may well feel that outsiders who do not belong to their private clubs, people who are "Independent" of their private clubs and have no investment in them, should not be able to barge into their clubs and have a say in selecting the leaders and other officials of their clubs. If you want to have a say in choosing the officers and leaders of the club, they say, then join the club. Become a member. Then you have a vested interest in who the officers of the club might be.

When it comes to political clubs, however, many voters, especially younger voters, have decided that they don't want to belong to any club whatsoever. They want to remain "Independent" of clubs. Indeed, many disdain the political clubs and scorn them, not wishing to be tainted by association with them.

Very well, the members of the clubs say. If you don't want to be a member of the club, then don't wail about "disenfranchisement" when we have elections for the leaders of our club. You can't have it both ways. You can either be a member of our private club, and vote for our rules and our officers, or you can keep your distance from our club.

But, if the latter, then don't try to barge into our private club when we elect our club officers and try to participate. In other words, if you want to have a say in choosing the Democratic presidential candidate, join the club. Register as a Democrat and become a member of the Democratic Party. Register as a Republican and become a member of the Republican Party.

If, however, you still believe you should not be required to be a member of the private club to choose the leaders of that private club, then you must change the state legislators who have said that's how it works in your state.

Those are the Rules of the Game when it comes to primary elections in America.

The Deep State:
The Fourth Branch of Government

Every four years political progressives engage in a debate over whether they should vote for "the lesser evil" candidate of the Democratic Party or cast an ideologically pure vote for a minor party candidate, such as the Green Party's champion.

Invariably, the debate swirls around the perceived personal and political inadequacies of the particular Democratic candidate. Far better, purists argue, to vote for what you want, and not get it, than vote for what you don't want, and actually get it. Further, if enough people cast the ideologically pure vote, someday in the distant future progressives may finally achieve "a party of our own," one of which they can be proud.

Unfortunately, given the constitutional constraints that structure the American political system, that far future day of ideological purity will never come, no matter how energetic and militant its advocates may be. Because of the way the Constitution mandates the election of our representatives, we are the only advanced democracy in the world that does not operate under a parliamentary or proportional representation electoral system. We operate under a winner-take-all electoral system based in geographical districts. (In the case of the Senate, the district is the state.)

Thus, you need 50.1% of the vote to win in a two-candidate race, and if you win, you get 100% of the political power. If you get 49.9% of the vote, you get nothing. This mandates a two-party system of ideologically "Big Tent" parties that struggle to straddle the broad middle in order to win a majority of the vote.

Meanwhile, ideologically pure parties of the Left and Right win nothing, no matter how dedicated their advocates. (If energy and sustained dedication were enough to sustain and grow a minor party into a major party, the Socialist Party would have grown into a major party in the early years of the twentieth century.)

However, even given the necessity of creating a broad coalition of ideologically impure voters in order to win anything at all, a greatly important difference has nevertheless evolved between our two major parties, regardless of who the presidential candidates might be in any given election. This is the difference between the Democratic Party's basic belief that government exists to serve the people and the Republican Party's belief that government is, at best, only a necessary evil, and that the main task of office holders is to dismantle the government. This is because, they argue, "The best government is the least government." And, by curtailing government power, they will be more able to reward the wealthy and large corporations, their ultimate economic agenda, regardless of their cultural or racial agendas.

This difference has vast implications for which party wins the White House. This is because the presidency is more than a single person, with his or her political beliefs and values. Instead, it is a vast executive bureaucracy, composed of tens of thousands of people, affecting almost every aspect of our lives.

Officially, the Constitution created three branches of government: The judicial, comprised of the Supreme Court; the legislative, comprised of both houses of Congress; and the executive, comprised of the presidency. The executive bureaucracy, however, all those employees and appointees of the executive branch, comprises in itself an unofficial fourth branch of government, what political conservatives malign as "The Deep State."

And, because the two major parties have vastly different attitudes toward that fourth branch of government, which party wins and controls that fourth branch has major implications. If they are Democratic employees and appointees, they will spend their time in office delivering government services and fulfilling the obligations their office or department was created to fulfill.

If they are Republican appointees, they will spend their time in office obstructing government services and trying to dismantle the "Deep State," very office or department they control.

This fourth branch is comprised, for example, of federally appointed judges throughout the land tasked with interpreting the law, and federally appointed U.S. Attorneys, tasked with enforcing labor laws, or, instead, if appointed by Republicans, spending much of their time investigating putative voter fraud.

Beyond the Department of Justice, there is every other Department for which there is a Cabinet Secretary, and all the tens of thousands of government servants under the jurisdiction of that Secretary. There are the workers in the Environmental Protection

Agency and the Federal Communications Commission, there are workers in the Department of Housing and Urban Development and the Department of the Interior. In a myriad of federal departments and federal agencies (such as the National Labor Relations Board, which oversees the National Labor Relations Act), thousands of employees make thousands of decisions affecting the delivery or non-delivery of governmental services to millions of Americans. These are decisions about consumer safety and scientific research, about civil rights and labor rights, about the protection of public lands and environmental pollution, about financial regulation and which swindling corporations to investigate, or not investigate. All of these positions are filled by the person who sits in the Oval Office.

Thus, the question of which party controls the "Deep State," the fourth branch of government, goes far beyond which person actually occupies the White House. It goes beyond whether health care will be introduced and perhaps extended. It goes beyond who will nominate judges to the U.S. Supreme Court over the next four to eight years, important as all these are. Depending on which party controls the fourth branch will mean the difference between whether the functionaries of the fourth branch will people who believe in carrying out the mission of their agency, or people who believe in subverting the mission of their agency. This is a life or death decision for millions of Americans, especially poorer Americans who, literally, cannot afford to be ideologically pure.

To this day, Ralph Nader, the Green Party presidential candidate in 2000, has no regrets about pulling enough votes away from the Democratic Party in Florida that year to give the state, and the White

House, to Republican George W. Bush. This is because he argues that there is no real difference between the two major parties. Beyond the fact that President Al Gore would not have invaded Iraq in 2003, thus creating the current chaos in the Middle East, there is another, very real, difference between the two major parties. This is the difference between the belief that government should serve the people, and the belief that government should be subverted and dismantled. Regardless of who the nominees may be in any particular election, the Democratic Party believes the former and the Republican Party believes the latter.

The reality is that either the Democratic Party or the Republican Party will win the presidential election in any election year and control the fourth branch of government. Since I believe that government exists to serve the people, and I want the the Deep State to work for me, and not against me, I vote for the Democratic Party, regardless of its presidential candidate in any particular election.

How To Change the World

Physicist Max Planck noted in his 1949 memoir, *A Scientific Autobiography*, that, "A new scientific truth does not triumph by convincing its opponents and making them see the light, but rather because its opponents eventually die, and a new generation grows up that is familiar with it."

This observation also helps explain how the world changes in general. It changes not by the conversion of opponents, by the winning of their hearts and minds, but by finding new adherents whose minds aren't already made up, whose minds are free from the weight of tradition.

Thomas Kuhn, who gave us the phrase and concept of "paradigm shifts" in his influential 1962 book, *The Structure of Scientific Revolutions*, agreed with this model of change. If any man can be said to have changed the world, surely it was Nicholas Copernicus, who replaced the geocentric Ptolemaic view of the heavens with a heliocentric view, arguing that the Sun, not the Earth, was at the center of the "Solar" System. And yet, noted Kuhn, "Copernicanism made few converts for almost a century after Copernicus' death. Newton's work was not generally accepted, particularly on the Continent, for more than half a century after the *Principia* appeared. Priestly never accepted the oxygen theory, nor Lord Kelvin the electromagnetic theory, and so on. The difficulties of conversion have often been noted by scientists themselves. Darwin, in a particularly perceptive passage at the end of his *Origin of Species*, wrote, 'I by no means expect to convince experienced naturalists whose minds are stocked with a multitude of facts all viewed, during a long course of years, from a point of view directly opposite to mine.... But I look with confidence to the future, to young and rising naturalists, who will be able to view both sides of the question with impartiality.'" As Kuhn notes, "These facts and others like them are too commonly known to need further emphasis."

But the world does not change only through the succession of generations. It also changes by reaching new audiences, those not already committed to an opposing point of view. This was something even Jesus of Nazareth, the Son of God, realized. Many Christians sometimes forget that Jesus was born a Jew, lived and taught among Jews, thought of himself as a Jew, and died a Jew. However, he taught that he was a special Jew. He was the Messiah, the long-prophesized Savior of Jewish tradition bringing salvation to the Jewish people.

Unfortunately, those who knew him best, the people of Nazareth, among whom he was born and raised, did not believe this about him. When he returned to his boyhood home to preach, a mob rejected him and drove him away. This moved him to remark bitterly upon how a prophet went unrecognized and unhonored among his own people.

Therefore, he went elsewhere seeking followers, among those not already doubting his destiny. In the Sea of Galilee port village of Magdala he found Mary (the) Magdalene, his most faithful convert, who followed him even to the Cross and the tomb. In the nearby village of Bethsaida, also

41

overlooking the Sea of Galilee, Jesus found more who knew him not, and therefore were receptive to his message. It was in Bethsaida that many testified to the miracles that Jesus was said to have performed. It was in Bethsaida that he healed a blind man and multiplied the loaves and fishes to feed the thousands who came to hear him preach. Many, watching from Bethsaida, saw him walk on the water of Galilee and calm the stormy waters with a word. And it was from among the fishermen of the tiny village of Bethsaida, where people knew him not, that Jesus found five of his most devoted disciples: James, John, Andrew, Philip, and, most devout of all, Peter, "the father of the church."

This is not to say that hearts and minds are never won. Sometimes dramatic conversions do occur, but perhaps their very rarity is what makes them so memorable. One of the most notable, so much so that it became a metaphor for dramatic conversion, was the transformation Saul of Tarsus underwent on the Road to Damascus. Saul was a Jew born in the Cilician city of Tarsus. He received his final religious education in Jerusalem, where he rose to a position of eminence as a Pharisee, a Jewish sect the New Testament portrays as opposed to Jesus and the early Christian movement. He may also have become a member of the Sanhedrin, the judicial and administrative court responsible for collecting Roman taxes and enforcing Roman laws.

As the followers of Jesus multiplied in Jerusalem following his death, Saul took personal responsibility for exterminating them. But, on the Road to Damascus, Syria, chasing Jewish Christians who had fled there, he experienced a remarkable vision which he compared to the appearance of Jesus to the disciples following his Resurrection. From a persecutor of Christians Saul, who now called himself "Paul", became their principal champion.

However, the vast majority of his fellow Jews was no more willing to accept Jesus as the Messiah than Paul had been previously. Therefore, Paul took his good news, his "gospel", outside Israel to the gentiles beyond, to those who had not already made up their minds about Jesus. He established and led many Christian churches in Asia Minor and Greece and the followers of Jesus spread throughout the Roman Empire.

The world is changed by the passage of time, as younger generations come of age in the midst of the debate, and whose minds are not already made up. And the world is changed by finding a new audience and gaining their adherence to your worldview.

So, forget about changing hearts and minds. Find a new audience. Take your message to the gentiles.

Solidarity

In the Garden of Gethsemane, Jesus told his disciple Peter, the devoted "rock" upon which he declared he would build his church, that Peter would disown him in the coming crisis on the morrow. "Not I," answered Peter, "never."

"Yes," said Jesus. "Before the cock crows you will deny me thrice."

Again Peter denied this.

Then, while his disciples slept nearby, Jesus suffered his own Dark Night of the Soul and doubted his ability to carry through what he knew he must soon do. But, he accepted the cup from which he must drink.

And then Roman soldiers, led by Judas, burst into the garden. They arrested Jesus and took him away. Fearful of a round up of suspected Jesus-followers, his disciples quickly scattered to their various dark corners and bolt holes.

Peter found himself alone, on a strange street, surrounded by hostile strangers. "There's one now!" cried one of the strangers, pointing at Peter. "Get him! He's a follower of Jesus!"

"No, not I," cried the frightened Peter. "I don't even know the man."

"Yes," cried the stranger, as the angry mob crowded around Peter, "you're a follower of Jesus, I saw you with him!"

"No, not me, you're mistaken, I don't even know the man!"

"Yes, it was you I saw with him, you're the one!

"No," cried Peter for the third time, "I tell you I don't even know the man!" And then, in fright, he ran away, and the mob let him go.

And then the cock crowed as a new day dawned.

Moral: Awake, alone, in the Garden of Gethsemane, even Jesus, who had become a mere man, come to suffer and die as a mere man, doubted himself, as a mere man might do, and prayed that he would not have to do what he had to do. But, he was, after all, also the Son of God, and he finally accepted the coming suffering and death that he knew he must face alone.

But the devoted Peter, only a mere man, was made of weaker stuff. And when he faced the crisis alone, he faltered and failed and denied he ever knew Jesus. Isolation makes cowards of us all, even if you're St. Peter.

The Long View

Movements for social and political change are always difficult and long and, often, defeated. It is easy for Movement activists to become disillusioned and demoralized in the wake of defeat.

But it is important for us to take the long view, and remind ourselves that, in politics, no matter how definitive they appear, there are no permanent defeats. Movements are like people, they age and they die.

But, new Movements, like new people, spring up and carry on the struggle. Battles are won and lost, and then are fought again under new names by new people. Rust never sleeps, power never sleeps, but no victory, and no defeat, is ever permanent.

Karl Marx and Frederick Engels famously said that the history of humanity is the history of class conflict. They were right, up to a point. But they thought history would come to an end with the final victory of the proletarians, the working class, and that victory would then abolish class conflict.

But there is no such final conflict; there is no end to the struggle. The road goes ever onward, and the journey is never-ending.

So take solace in the struggle, in the journey, for you will meet new and unexpected companions on that fantastic never-ending road trip.

And there will *always* be new companions.

Eric Leif Davin, Ph.D., is the author of *The Great Strike of 1877; Crucible of Freedom: Workers' Democracy in the Industrial Heartland, 1914-1960; Radicals in Power: The New Left Experience in Office*; *A Forlorn Hope: Third Parties and American Political Ideology*, and, with Staughton Lynd, *Picket Line and Ballot Box: The Forgotten Legacy of the Labor Party Movement, 1932-1936*.

He is also the author of *The Paterson Strike Pageant: An IWW Novel of Bohemia and Insurgent Labor; Solidarity: An IWW Novel of the Steel City*, and *The Year of Hope and Fear: Insurrection and Repression, 1919*.

His essay, "The Very Last Hurrah: The Defeat of the Labor Party Idea, 1934-1936," appeared in *"We Are All Leaders: The Alternative Unionism of the Early 1930s,"* (University of Illinois Press, 1996), edited by Staughton Lynd. It won the Eugene V. Debs Foundation's prize as the best essay of that year reflecting the enduring spirit of Eugene V. Debs.

www.ingramcontent.com/pod-product-compliance
Lightning Source LLC
Chambersburg PA
CBHW050348290526
45785CB00006B/2686